EXPLORING WITH SELAM & SENAI
LET'S LEARN AMHARIC!

Written by Semhar Woldeslassie

Illustrated by Alem Derege

Exploring with Selam & Senai
Let's Learn Amharic!

Text and Illustrations copyright © 2021 Semhar Woldeslassie

All rights reserved. No part of this publication may be reproduced, distributed, or transmitted in any form or by any means, including photocopying, recording, or other electronic or mechanical methods, without the prior written permission of the publisher, except in case of brief quotations embodied in critical reviews and certain other than noncommercial uses permitted by copyright law. For permission requests, write to the publisher, addressed "Attention: Permissions Coordinator," at exploringwithselamxsenai@gmail.com.

Published by Semhar Woldeslassie
Cover design and illustrations by Alem Derege

Translated to Amharic by family and friends

www.exploringwithselamxsenai.com
First Printing, 2021.

To my family and friends, thank you for your support. I am forever indebted to you.

To my nieces and nephews, thank you for being my inspiration. May you always remember that there is no limit to what you can accomplish.

To the beautiful souls reading this, may you never forget that your true superpower stems from learning about your history, culture, and language.

- S.W.

Hi! It's Selam and Senai. We're twins. We live with our mom, dad, and two older siblings. The favorite in the family is our dog, Teddy. We begged our parents for years to adopt a dog. Our grandparents still don't approve. Everytime grandma sees Teddy, she shouts, *"hid kezih."* We like learning our traditional language Amharic with our family. Come along and learn with us!

We love being mommy's little helpers in the kitchen. She teaches us how to cook and clean. Mommy makes the best *kita firfir* in the world. We help her make *shayi* for the guests.

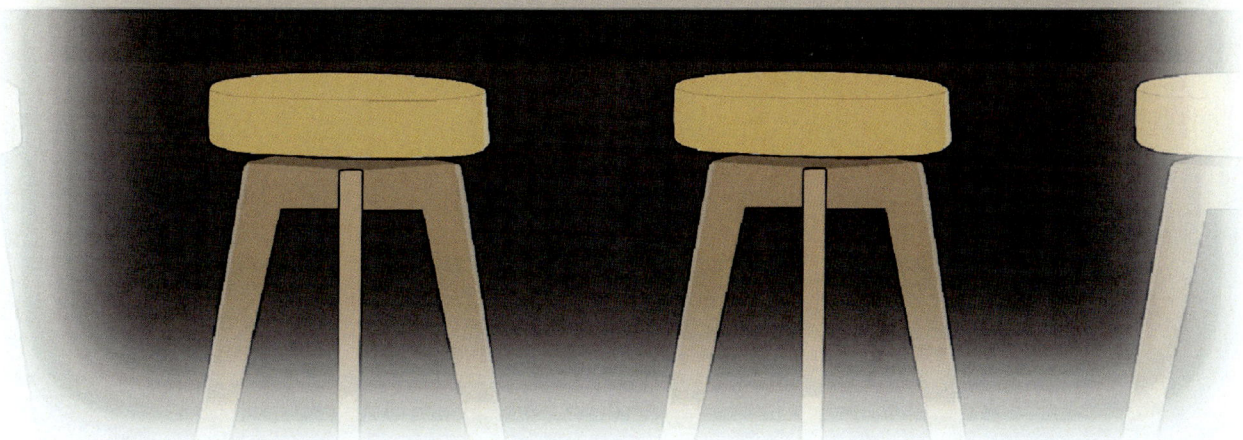

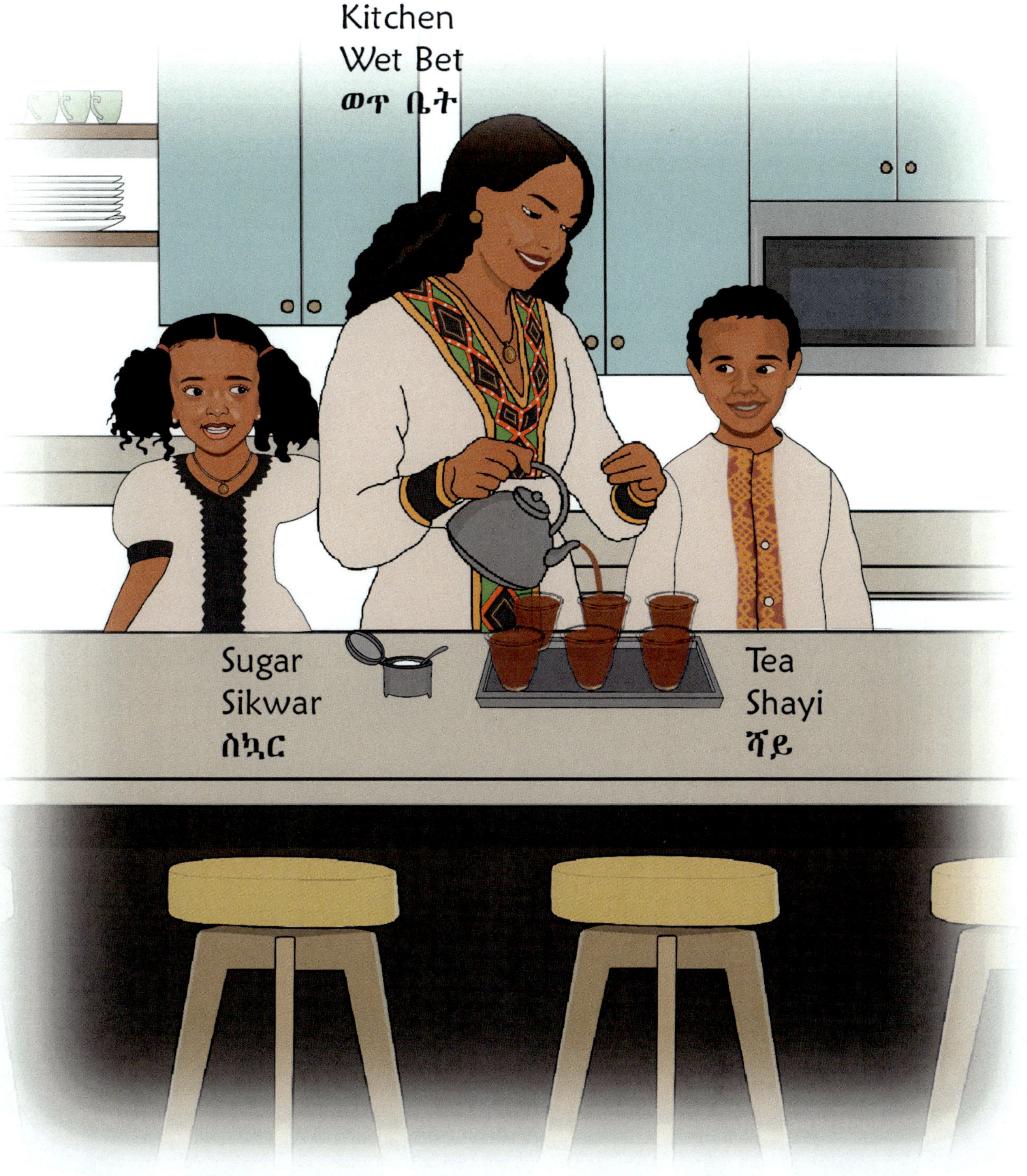
Kitchen
Wet Bet
ወጥ ቤት
Sugar
Sikwar
ስኳር
Tea
Shayi
ሻይ

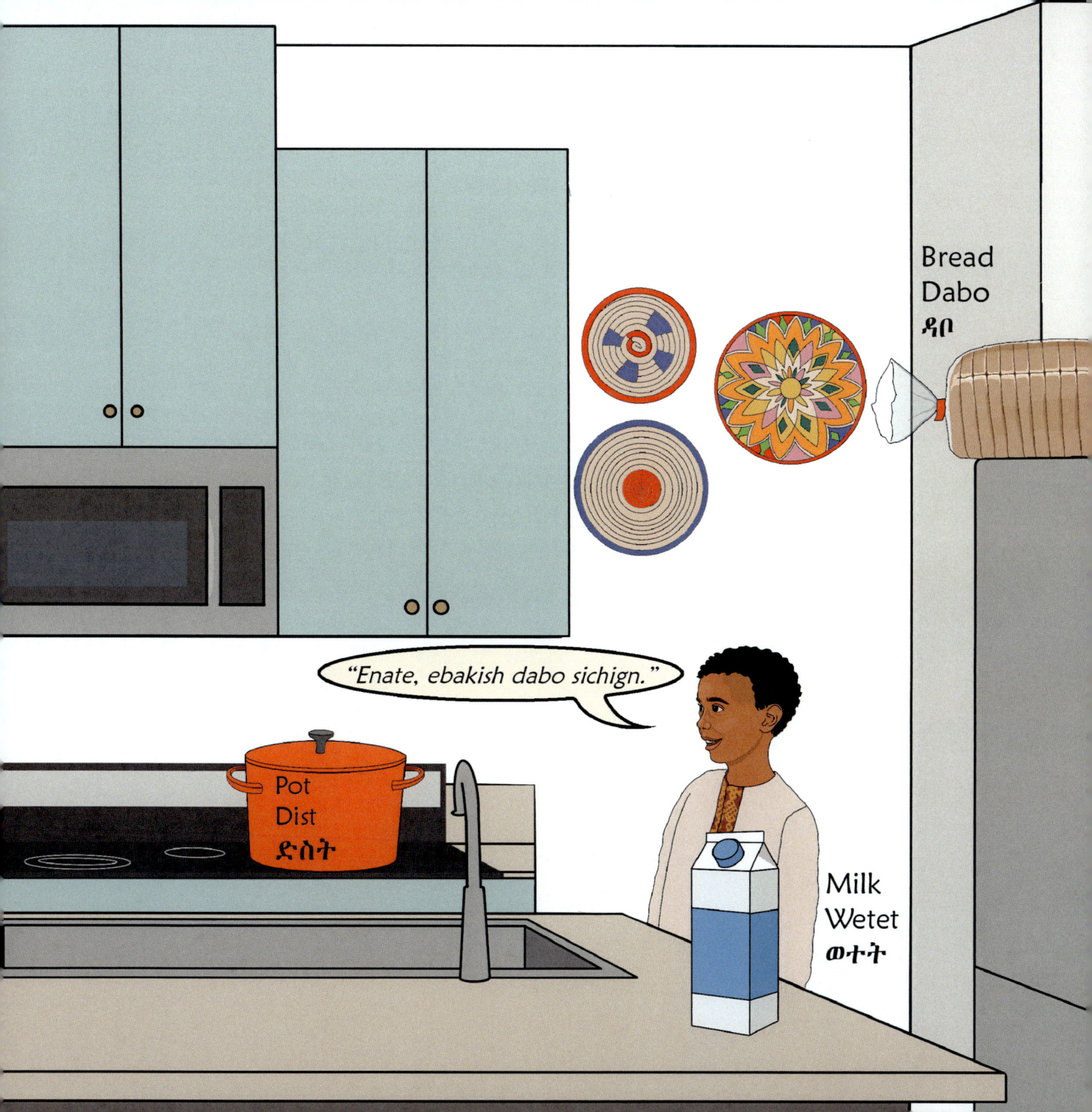

We love visiting the zoo with our dad. He teaches us about different animals. Our favorite animal is the giraffe. Going to the zoo is always a lot of fun. He's the best dad in the world.

We enjoy spending time with our big brother and sister. Our brother is goofy and makes us laugh. Our sister comes up with lots of fun activities for us to do as a family, such as game nights and movie nights. We like playing Simon Says in Amharic.

Grandpa likes sitting on the porch to watch us play outside. We enjoy playing with our toys and riding our bikes around the neighborhood. Grandpa makes sure that we are safe while playing outside.

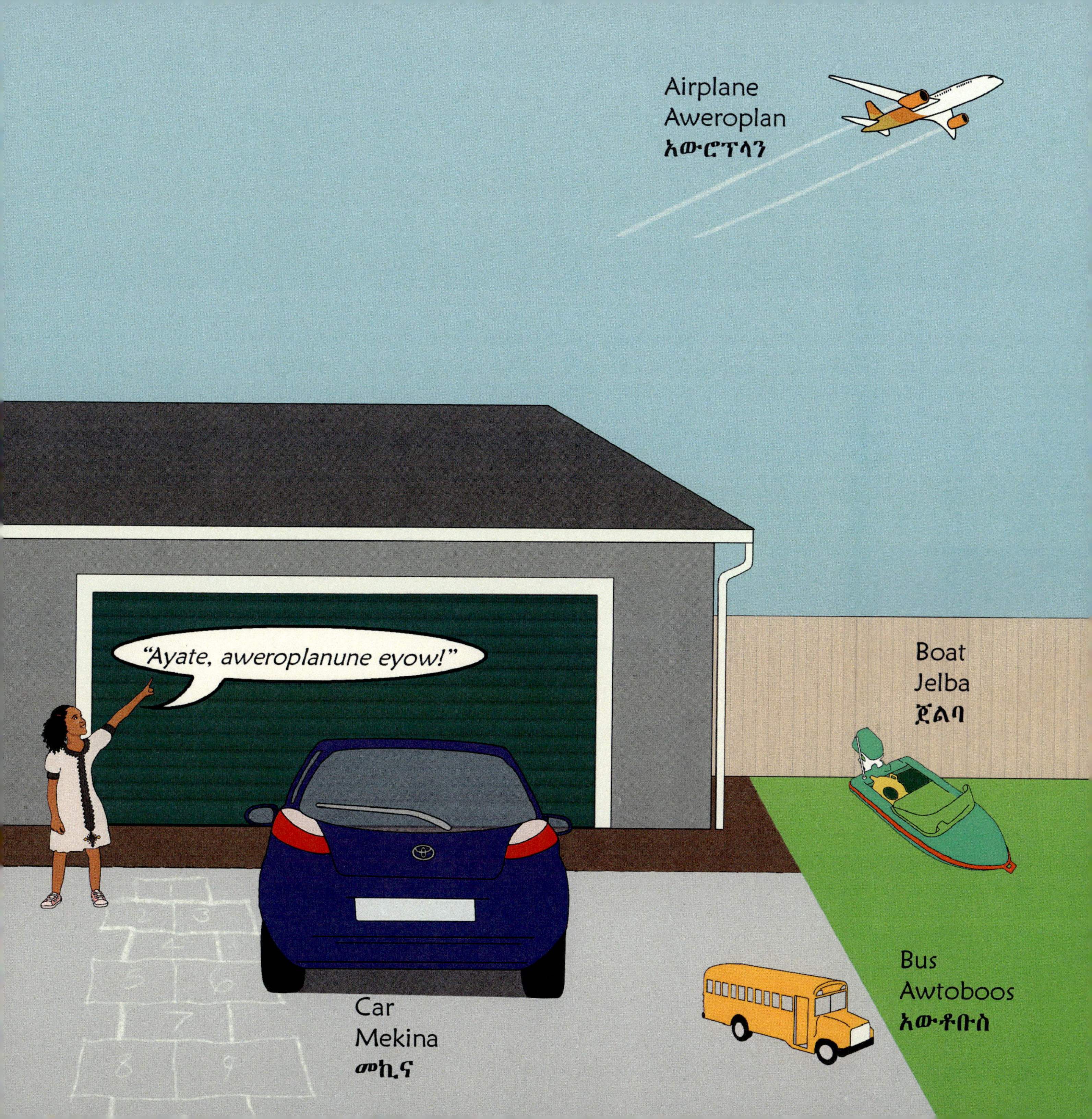
Airplane
Aweroplan
አውሮፕላን
"Ayate, aweroplanune eyow!"
Boat
Jelba
ጀልባ
Car
Mekina
መኪና
Bus
Awtoboos
አውቶቡስ

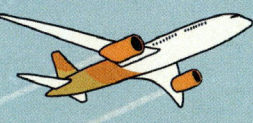

Grandma loves making *buna* for our family. *Buna* is a cultural coffee ceremony. We like being grandma's *buna* helpers. We pass out the *ambasha* and *fendisha*. She pours milk in our *yebuna sini* to include us in the ceremony, since we're too young to drink coffee. This makes us feel special. While drinking *buna*, she teaches us how to introduce ourselves in Amharic.
Are you ready to learn?

Selam! *(Hi)* ሰላም

Indet nachu? *(How's everybody doing?)* እንዴት ናችሁ?

Simae_____ yebalale. *(My name is ___.)* ስሜ _____ ይባላል።

Edmeye ____amet newe. *(I'm ___ years old.)* እድሜዬ _____ ዓመት ነው።

Yenate sim ____ yebalale. *(My mother's name is ___.)* የናቴ ስም _____ ይባላል።

Yebate sim ____ yebalale. *(My father's name is ___.)* ያባቴ ስም _____ ይባላል።

Ene yemenorwe _____ newe. *(I live in ___.)* እኔ የምኖረው _____ ነው።

Ameseginalehu! *(Thank you!)* አመሰግናለሁ።

Thank you for learning Amharic with us.
We'll see you on our next adventure!

Glossary

"Hid kezih"	"Go away"
Kita firfir / Chechebsa	Traditional breakfast dish
Yebuna Sini	Traditional coffee ceremony cups
Ambasha	Traditional bread
Fendisha	Popcorn
"Enate, ebakish dabo sichign"	"Mother, please give me bread"
"Ayate, aweroplanune eyow"	"Grandpa, look at the plane"
"Ayate, tiru buna"	"Grandma, good coffee"

Made in the USA
Las Vegas, NV
02 June 2024